SUPER COOL
CHEMICAL REACTION
ACTIVITIES

WITH MAX AXIOM

by Agnieszka Biskup

Consultant:
Bridget Alligood DePrince, Ph.D.
Department of Chemistry and Biochemistry
Florida State University, Tallahassee

Graphic Library is published by Capstone Press,
1710 Roe Crest Drive, North Mankato, Minnesota 56003
www.capstonepub.com

Library of Congress Cataloging-in-Publication Data

Biskup, Agnieszka, author.
 Super cool chemical reaction activities with Max Axiom / by Agnieszka
Biskup.
     pages cm.—(Graphic library. Max Axiom science and engineering
activities)
 Includes bibliographical references and index.
 Summary: "Super Scientist, Max Axiom, presents step-by-step photo
Illustrated instructions for conducting a variety of chemical reaction
experiments and activities"—Provided by publisher.
 Audience: 8-14.
 Audience: Grade 4 to 6.
 ISBN 978-1-4914-2077-5 (library binding)
 ISBN 978-1-4914-2281-6 (paperback)
 ISBN 978-1-4914-2295-3 (eBook PDF)

1. Chemical reactions—Experiments—Juvenile literature. 2. Chemical
reactions—Experiments—Comic books, strips, etc. 3. Graphic novels. I. Title.
 QD502.B56 2015
 541'.39078—dc23   2014027882

Editor
Christopher L. Harbo

Art Director
Nathan Gassman

Designer
Tracy McCabe

Production Specialist
Katy LaVigne

Cover Illustration
Marcelo Baez

Project Creation
Sarah Schuette and Marcy Morin

Photographs by Capstone Studio:
Karon Dubke

Printed in the United States of
America in Stevens Point,
Wisconsin.
042016   009711R

Table of Contents

Chemical reactions are all around us. Some reactions we don't control, such as the flash of a firefly.

But others we *can* actually control, such as burning wood or setting off fireworks.

In a chemical reaction, one substance changes into a new substance.

This fire changes wood into ash and smoke. It may seem like magic, but it's real!

BUBBLING BLOBS

Oil and water don't mix, and this project uses that fact to its advantage. Check out how a chemical reaction can create a super cool lava lamp.

YOU'LL NEED

clear, clean plastic 16.9-oz. (500-mL) drink bottle

vegetable oil

water

food coloring

effervescent tablets

PLAN OF ACTION

1. Fill the bottle three-fourths full of vegetable oil. Then slowly pour water into the bottle until it's almost full.

2. Wait a few minutes for the oil and water to separate completely.

3. Add about 12 drops of food coloring.

4. Wait for the food coloring to fall through the oil and mix with the water on the bottom.

5. Break an effervescent tablet into three or four pieces, and drop them into the bottle.

6. Watch the blobs begin to rise!

⚡ AXIOM EXPLANATION

The effervescent tablet reacts with the colored water to form bubbles of carbon dioxide gas. The gas rises and takes some of the colored water with it. The gas escapes when it reaches the top of the bottle. The colored water droplets then fall back down into the bottle.

effervescent—bubbling, hissing, or foaming as gas escapes

carbon dioxide—a colorless, odorless gas

ENDOTHERMIC BAGGIES

Some chemical reactions absorb energy and decrease the temperature of their surrounding environment. Try this experiment to feel the effects of an **endothermic reaction** as it happens in the palm of your hand.

YOU'LL NEED

1 teaspoon (5 mL) citric acid*

1 teaspoon (5 mL) baking soda

1-quart (1-liter) zipper-type plastic storage bag

water

*found at health food stores or at supermarkets with canning supplies

1. Pour the citric acid and baking soda into the plastic bag.

Baking Soda

Citric Acid

2. Shake the bag gently to mix the two ingredients.

3. Pour a small amount of water into the bag and seal it quickly.

4. Hold the bag in the palm of your hand as the chemical reaction takes place.

⚡ AXIOM EXPLANATION

Citric acid, baking soda, and water react to produce carbon dioxide. The gas fills and inflates the bag. Because the reaction is endothermic, the liquid in the bag becomes cold to the touch. Once the reaction ends, the mixture returns to room temperature.

endothermic reaction—a chemical reaction that absorbs energy from its surroundings

acid—a substance that will react with a base to form a salt; strong acids can burn a person's skin

MONSTER TOOTHPASTE

When it comes to chemical reactions, the most exciting ones are often **exothermic reactions**. They can produce energy as heat—sometimes in surprising ways. Monster toothpaste is one exothermic reaction that never fails to wow a crowd.

YOU'LL NEED

small bowl

packet of dry yeast

3 tablespoons (45 mL) of warm water

clear plastic drink bottle

foil roasting pan

½ cup (118 mL) of 6% hydrogen peroxide*

liquid dish soap

food coloring

funnel

*found in beauty supply stores or hair salons

SAFETY FIRST

Put on gloves and safety goggles before trying this experiment. Hydrogen peroxide can irritate eyes and exposed skin.

PLAN OF ACTION

1. Mix the yeast and warm water in a small bowl.

2. Set the mixture aside for about 30 seconds, or until the liquid becomes frothy.

3. Place the plastic bottle upright in the center of the roasting pan. Ask an adult to pour the hydrogen peroxide into the bottle.

4. Put two or three squirts of liquid dish soap into the bottle.

5. Add about 5 drops of food coloring to the bottle.

6. Gently swirl the bottle to mix the ingredients and return it to the center of the pan.

7. Using the funnel, pour the yeast solution from step 1 into the bottle.

8. Quickly remove the funnel, stand back, and watch the monster toothpaste ooze out!

⚡ AXIOM EXPLANATION

The yeast speeds up the chemical reaction that breaks hydrogen peroxide into oxygen gas and water. The dish soap traps the oxygen, resulting in the formation of foam bubbles. The foam is basically soap and water, so it's safe to touch. Because this is an exothermic reaction, the bottle and foam should feel warm.

exothermic reaction—a chemical reaction that releases energy to its surroundings

MINI MAGIC FIRE EXTINGUISHER

A fire will keep burning as long as it has fuel, oxygen, and heat. This chemical reaction removes one of those ingredients to put out a fire.

YOU'LL NEED

3 votive candles

matches

2-quart (2-liter) clear glass pitcher

2 tablespoons (30 mL) of baking soda

1 cup (225 mL) vinegar

SAFETY FIRST

Be sure to ask an adult for help using candles and matches before doing this activity.

PLAN OF ACTION

1. Place the candles in a row on a flat surface in an open area outside. Ask an adult to use the matches to light the candles.

2. Place the baking soda into the pitcher.

3. Pour in the vinegar. Swirl the pitcher so that the ingredients are well mixed. The mixture will fizz and foam.

4. Slowly tip the pitcher near the candles without spilling any liquid. Watch what happens to the candle flames.

⚡ AXIOM EXPLANATION

When vinegar and baking soda mix, the chemical reaction forms carbon dioxide gas. Carbon dioxide is heavier than air, so it will stay in the pitcher longer while it's upright. When the pitcher is tipped over the flames, the carbon dioxide pours out. It sinks down over the candles, pushing the oxygen out of the way. The flames go out because a fire can't burn without oxygen.

EGG-CELLENT EGGSPERIMENT

What does an egg look like without a shell? Find out with a chemical reaction with the power to make an eggshell disappear.

YOU'LL NEED

1 raw egg

clear glass jar with lid

vinegar

flashlight

1. Gently place the egg in the jar.

2. Add enough vinegar to completely cover the egg. Screw the lid on the jar.

3. Let the egg sit in the vinegar for 24 hours at room temperature.

4. Use the lid of the jar to gently strain the vinegar into a sink. Be careful to not let the egg fall out of the jar.

5. Cover the egg with fresh vinegar, and let it sit undisturbed for another two days.

6. Carefully remove the egg from the vinegar. Gently rinse it with water.

7. Shine a flashlight through the rubbery egg to see the yolk.

AXIOM EXPLANATION

You may have noticed tiny bubbles all over the egg in the vinegar. These bubbles were carbon dioxide gas. They were produced by a chemical reaction between the vinegar and the egg shell. Vinegar, which contains acetic acid, reacted with the eggshell to dissolve it.

Bones are hard and typically break if you try to bend them. This chemical reaction will give you bones that behave in funny ways.

YOU'LL NEED

1 or 2 chicken bones

clear glass jar with lid

vinegar

PLAN OF ACTION

I. Rinse and clean the bones with warm water to make sure all the meat has been removed.

2. Let the bones dry. Note that the bones are hard and do not bend.

3. Place the bones in a jar.

4. Add vinegar to the jar to completely cover the bones. Place the lid on the jar.

5. Let the bones sit for at least 3 days.

6. Remove the bones from the vinegar.

7. Try to bend the bones now. Do they feel any different?

AXIOM EXPLANATION

Bones contain calcium and phosphorus. These minerals make bones strong and hard. The acetic acid in the vinegar reacts with the minerals. It leaves the remaining materials in the bone soft and rubbery.

calcium—a soft, silver-white mineral found in teeth and bones

phosphorus—a mineral in the body found most in teeth and bones

POLISHED PENNIES AND COPPER NAILS

Have you ever noticed that pennies turn darker with age? It's all because of chemical reactions. In this two-part experiment, you'll make some old pennies look new again while turning others a little green! You'll also make a steel nail look like copper.

YOU'LL NEED

glass or plastic bowl (not metal)

¼ cup (60 mL) of vinegar

1 teaspoon (5 mL) of salt

plastic spoon

20 old, dirty copper pennies*

paper towels

marker

kitchen timer

2 clean steel nails

*For best results, use pennies minted before 1982—they contain more copper than pennies today.

PLAN OF ACTION PART ONE

1. Pour the vinegar into the bowl.

2. Add the salt to the vinegar, and stir it with a plastic spoon until the salt dissolves.

3. Put all the pennies in the bowl.

4. Wait about 5 minutes, then take all the pennies out of the bowl. They should look shiny. Set the bowl of vinegar aside for part two of this experiment.

5. Place 10 of the pennies on a paper towel to dry.

6. Rinse the other 10 pennies under running water, and place them on another paper towel to dry. Write "rinsed" on that paper towel with a marker so you know which is which.

7. Set the kitchen timer for 1 hour and leave your rinsed pennies to dry. In the meantime, proceed to part two of this experiment.

continued

1. Submerge one steel nail into the leftover salt/vinegar liquid.

2. Place the other steel nail half-in and half-out of the liquid by leaning it against the side of the bowl.

3. Let the nails sit for the remainder of the time left on the kitchen timer you set in part one.

4. When the timer goes off, check to see how your pennies and nails look.

AXIOM EXPLANATION

New pennies turn a dirty brown over time because copper reacts with oxygen in the air. A dark substance called copper oxide forms on the surface. The acetic acid in the vinegar removes the copper oxide from the pennies, making them bright and shiny again.

Rinsing the pennies under water stops the chemical reaction. The salt/vinegar mix left on the unrinsed pennies allows the chemical reaction to continue, forming a blue-green chemical coating.

The vinegar/salt solution removed some of the copper from the pennies, which remains in the liquid. When the steel nails are placed in the liquid, the copper is attracted to the metal of the nail. You end up with copper-coated nails!

LACTIC PLASTIC

In the early 1900s, **casein** plastic was used for jewelry, buttons, combs, and buckles. Surprisingly, this plastic was made with ordinary cow's milk. With a simple chemical reaction, you can make your very own casein plastic.

YOU'LL NEED

1 cup (225 mL) of whole milk

small pot

small bowl

4 teaspoons (20 mL) of vinegar

food coloring

spoon

fine mesh strainer

large bowl

paper towels

casein—a type of protein found in milk

continued

PLAN OF ACTION

1. Ask an adult to heat the milk in a pot on the stove. Heat until the milk is very hot but not boiling.

2. Have an adult pour the hot milk into a small bowl.

3. Add the vinegar and 5 drops of food coloring to the milk.

4. Stir the mixture slowly with a spoon for about a minute.

5. Carefully pour the milk through the strainer into a larger bowl. A bunch of clumps should remain in the strainer. Pour any liquid in the bowl down the drain.

6. Let the clumps cool for a few minutes. Place them on a paper towel, and press them gently with another paper towel to soak up any extra moisture.

7. Knead the clumps together with your fingers to make a ball. You have just made a ball of casein plastic.

8. Mold your plastic into any shape you want.

9. Set your molded plastic on a plate to dry and harden for two days.

AXIOM EXPLANATION

Milk is full of a protein called casein. The combination of heat and acetic acid from the vinegar makes the milk curdle. This process pulls the casein proteins out of the milk to form rubbery clumps called curds. The casein curds make up the plastic you can form into various shapes.

protein—a chemical made by animal and plant cells to carry out various functions

GLUE GOO

Sometimes chemistry can get a little gooey. Create a homemade version of slime by using the power of cross-linking **molecules**!

YOU'LL NEED

2 plastic disposable cups

1 teaspoon (5 mL) of Borax powder*

½ cup (118 mL) of water

plastic spoon

½ cup (118 mL) of white craft glue

food coloring

glass bowl

*found at the supermarket near the laundry detergent

PLAN OF ACTION

1. Add the Borax powder and half of the water to a plastic cup. Stir well with the plastic spoon, then set aside.

2. Pour the glue into a second plastic cup.

3. Add the remaining water and a few drops of food coloring to the glue.

4. Use the plastic spoon to stir the glue-water mixture well.

5. Pour the contents of both cups into the bowl. Stir well. The slime will form before your very eyes.

6. Let it sit for about 30 seconds before you pull it out to play with it. Put the slime in a sealed plastic bag to keep it from drying out.

⚡ AXIOM EXPLANATION

White craft glue is a *polymer*. It is made up of long chains of molecules of a substance called polyvinyl acetate. The chains easily slip and slide against each other, allowing the glue to be poured. When you add the Borax and water solution to the glue, a chemical reaction occurs. The long glue molecule chains get cross-linked together to form the rubbery, stretchy, gooey stuff we call slime.

molecule—a group of two or more atoms bonded together; a molecule is the smallest part of a substance that can't be divided without a chemical change

polymer—a natural or synthetic compound made up of small, simple molecules linked together in long chains of repeating units

MAGIC COLOR CHANGE

Sometimes a chemical reaction can look like magic. This show-stopping experiment has an astounding color change that happens in the blink of an eye!

YOU'LL NEED

2 500-milligram vitamin C tablets*

plastic sandwich baggie

metal spoon

measuring spoons

3 disposable clear plastic cups, labeled "I," "2," and "3"

warm water

plastic spoons for stirring

I teaspoon (5 mL) of 2% tincture of iodine*

I tablespoon (15 mL) of 3% hydrogen peroxide*

½ teaspoon (2 mL) of liquid laundry starch

stopwatch

*find these items at a pharmacy or drugstore

SAFETY FIRST

Remember to wear safety goggles and gloves while handling iodine and hydrogen peroxide in this experiment.

1. Place the vitamin C tablets in a plastic baggie. Crush them into a fine powder using the back of a metal spoon.

2. Pour the crushed powder into Cup 1. Then add 4 tablespoons (60 mL) of warm water to the cup.

3. Stir for at least half a minute with a plastic spoon. The liquid may be cloudy.

4. Scoop 1 teaspoon (5 mL) of the liquid from Cup 1 and pour it into Cup 2.

continued

5. Add 4 tablespoons (60 mL) of warm water and the iodine to Cup 2. Did the brown iodine turn clear?

6. Add 4 tablespoons (60 mL) of warm water, the hydrogen peroxide, and the liquid laundry starch to Cup 3.

7. Pour all of the liquid from Cup 2 into Cup 3 and start your stopwatch. Now pour the liquid back and forth between Cup 3 and Cup 2 a few times.

8. Set the cup down on a table and watch the liquid. The colorless liquid will turn dark blue in a flash! Check your stopwatch to see how long the reaction took.

9. Now add 2 tablespoons (30 mL) of liquid from Cup 1 into the cup with blue liquid. Stir well. Your dark blue liquid will suddenly turn clear again!

⚡ AXIOM EXPLANATION

This experiment may seem like magic—but it's science. It is called an iodine clock reaction. Scientists use clock reactions to study the rates of chemical reactions. They can determine how fast *reactants* are used up or *products* appear.

When iodine and starch make contact, they react to form a new dark blue substance. But the vitamin C prevents the iodine from reacting with the starch. The color change will only occur after all the vitamin C is used up. This experiment is a chemical battle between the starch and the vitamin C. The starch wants to make the iodine blue. The vitamin C is trying to stop the blue reaction from happening at all!

reactant—a substance that undergoes a chemical change in a chemical reaction

product—the substances that are produced from a chemical reaction

Glossary

acid (ASS-id)—a substance that will react with a base to form a salt; strong acids can burn a person's skin

calcium (KAL-see-uhm)—a soft, silver-white mineral found in teeth and bones

carbon dioxide (KAHR-buhn dy-AHK-syd)—a colorless, odorless gas

casein (KAY-seen)—a type of protein found in milk

effervescent (ef-uhr-VESS-ent)—bubbling, hissing, or foaming as gas escapes

endothermic reaction (en-doh-THUR-mik ree-AK-shuhn)—a chemical reaction that absorbs energy from its surroundings

exothermic reaction (ex-oh-THUR-mik ree-AK-shuhn)—a chemical reaction that releases energy to its surroundings

molecule (MOL-uh-kyool)—a group of two or more atoms bonded together; a molecule is the smallest part of a substance that can't be divided without a chemical change

phosphorus (FOSS-fur-uhss)—a mineral in the body found most in teeth and bones

polymer (POL-uh-mur)—a natural or synthetic compound made up of small, simple molecules linked together in long chains of repeating units

product (PROD-uhkt)—the substances that are produced from a chemical reaction

protein (PROH-teen)—a chemical made by animal and plant cells to carry our various functions

reactant (ree-AK-tent)—a substance that undergoes a chemical change in a chemical reaction

Read More

Bateman, Graham. *Chemical Reactions.* Facts at Your Fingertips. Redding, Conn.: Brown Bear Books, 2010.

Cooper, Christopher E. *The Basics of Energy and Reactions.* Core Concepts. New York: Rosen Publishing, 2014.

Parker, Steve. *Crackling Chemistry*. Science Crackers. Irvine, Calif.: QEB Pub., 2011.

Internet Sites

FactHound offers a safe, fun way to find Internet sites related to this book. All of the sites on FactHound have been researched by our staff.

Here's all you do:

Visit *www.facthound.com*

Type in this code: 9781491420775

Check out projects, games and lots more at **www.capstonekids.com**

Index